WHAT'S TO BE DONE WITH BEAUTY

Lois Parker Edstrom

Published by creative justice press, 1249 Portage Road Kalamazoo, MI 49001

Cover art by Denise Miller
Cover design and book layout by Shawntai Brown and Denise Miller
Shawntai Brown and Denise Miller, editors
ISBN – 978-1-105-52423-3

Dedicated to my sons

Brian and Brent

For the joy that is mine because of you

TABLE OF CONTENTS

AMERICAN GOTHIC
Oil on Beaverboard, 1930
The Art Institute of Chicago

Grant Wood, look
what you've done to these people
constrained between pitchfork
and there beyond that gothic window,
beyond those trees,
the shadow of a steeple.

The unmarried daughter standing
slightly behind her father,
cameo at junction of white collar,
hears worried whispers
from the past, but along the slender
neck a wisp of hair escapes
your brush and her tending;
she can let it all down, desire
zig-zagging behind that shuttered gaze
like rick-rack on her apron.

And the father, the farmer
so solemn, tight-buttoned,
proper. He has lived
within the art, obedient
to your vision, his pockets filled
with mercy, and the work-hardened
hand remembers the tender
curve of his bride in night's light,
long ago, hungering behind
that lace curtain.

These two, the father
and the daughter, rise
from the oil, tint
and toil of their existence,
parting pigment, tracing
longings within rigid lines,
voices in undertone compelling
us to know, we are not
what we seem,
we are so much more.

PRIVATE MAN

The Dinner Horn
Oil on Canvas, 1870
Winslow Homer, 1836 - 1910
Private Collection

That young girl standing in sunlight,
The Dinner Horn pressed to her lips,
a crescent of dark striped underskirt revealed
beneath her soft white dress.
Is she calling to workers in the field
or to this reclusive artist who preferred
painting *en plein air*?

He held the details of his life in a tight fist,
releasing parts of himself
only when he picked up a brush,
filled, as he was, with light and shadow,
lines connecting the puzzle
of who he was.

How else those first paintings
to arrive fully formed?
Detail, like the perfection
of a fetal fingernail, the inner life
of his subjects emerging the way
nests appear when leaves forsake
the trees of winter.

POPPIES IN THE FOG
Photography by Mel Edstrom, 2010
Private Collection

Fog slips through the Straits of Juan de Fuca,
settles itself in Admiralty Inlet

and eases over our part of the island,
a cocooning of fields and house

until hard edges soften
like the easing of long held pain

and everything quiets down,
a private world where

what lies ahead is obscured
and we are satisfied

with not knowing.
The foghorn's muffled

lament, close then more distant;
a curious comfort and from the shore,

on the incoming tide, I see
a heron ghosting by on driftwood.

Now fog fills our gardens
where purple poppies cup

this fragile ration of sky
and silver dewdrops bead

the blooms, poise
on jade leaves, slide down

the stem of spent blossoms,
each pod a vault

of silent explosions.

THE GLEANERS

Oil on Canvas, 1857
Jean-Francois Millet, 1814 - 1875
Musee, d'Orsay, Paris

We don't know what to do
with the poor. There they are
in the midst of all that splendor

a cornucopia pouring
light on their bent backs
and the sheaves of wheat

clutched in work-worn hands.
At what price they labor to gain
so little. Weep, if you must,

but dare not spill sorrow
on their homespun bindings.
How is it possible to separate

the subtle shades of need
from hues of blessing,
a mélange of sweat and stubble.

Haystacks spiral skyward
like golden castles, and beyond
Paris, the Forest Fontainebleau;

a horizon to the next good thing.

GREEN APPLE ON BLACK PLATE

Oil on canvas, 1921
Georgia O'Keefe 1887 - 1986
Birmingham Art Museum, Alabama

You look upon this apple as a god –
reverential washing, one sacrificial slice
exposing moon-white halves,
four brown seeds cupped in translucent pods.
Then careful paring and separation,
thin green-rimmed crescents fanned on black plate-
communion offered to those of us who wait.

I consider past transgressions –
the pleasure of a lusty bite,
the crunch and slurp of apple gouged
by teeth and ravished to the core,
the stem and withered blossom end.

STILL LIFE
Oil on copper, 1942
Frida Kahlo,1907 - 1954

So the painting is controversial.
So the president's wife sent it back,
the commissioned piece meant

for an honored place in the palace.
So a friend acquired it.
Then it went missing.

This carefully arranged viscera
the anatomy of ripeness,
of life, of small deaths.

Fruits and vegetables
that somehow become
more than they are.

Fingered fronds wave
like sea anemones against
the teal background, float

and open, fallopian ballerinas
poised to net a seed, now implanted
in the squash's moist cavity.

Soft folds of bloom, gonadic plums,
the lime's distended nipple,
pale lips and the pear's puckered

blossom end. A Polyphemus moth
hovers above, seeks ripe flesh
to lay her eggs, then die.

After Frida's death
the painting was found,
hidden for years on the canopy

above her bed.

EDWARD HOPPER'S WOMEN

You watch them
at the automat,
an after hours office,
in motel rooms,
a train compartment
and in a dim *New York Movie*

you place a man who watches
with a distant woman
the flickering lives of others.
The usherette, drawn
into her own drama
sees the bloom of war,
heavy with blood-scent,
who will go, who will return.

Your skilled hands pare
A Woman in the Sun
to bareness
and I, like you,
become a voyeur
burned by what I see
smoldering beneath
the surface of the canvas.

The women, they look too;
we can't know
what they see.

LADIES WITH PARASOLS

Watercolor and pencil on paper, 1896 - 1897
Maurice Prendergast, 1858 - 1924
Private Collection

This day at the shore
heat rises like a serpent
undulating before a strike.

The two women don't quite belong
to themselves or each other,
their bodies contoured
in graphite and shadow,

a fine separation penciled
in Victorian suitability
beneath their long white dresses.

What brings them to water,
these two; daring red
parasols in the midst of pastels
and black-suited males.

One looks forward,
the other turns back
the heat rises, forms
its own distorted image.

They waver like a sea filled with tides.

HOLLYHOCKS
Oil on canvas, undated
Fredrick Frieseke 1874 - 1939
National Academy of Design, New York

"My one idea… is to produce the effect of vibration."

Hear the vibration of sunlight flickering
among hollyhocks, an indefinable pip

which plants itself in furrows of the brain
the way a seed, that casket of rebirth,

opens to amenable soil. The woman,
elegant as the garden, touches a flower –

a tuft of bells, a chiming swell,
striations of the heart

tremble, steal thunder
from the mouth.

What's to be done with beauty?

YOUNG WOMAN SEWING

Oil on canvas, 1886
Mary Cassatt 1844 - 1926
The Art Institute of Chicago

A young woman, cocooned in batiste,
dark eyelashes, hair pulled up exposing neck;
in her hands a cascade of delicate fabric,
and those fingers posed like Degas' dancers
ready to pinpoint the thrust of needle.

The dark river of her hat and silk scarf
brims at the headwaters and flows
down along the ridges of neck
across the mound of breast, over the heart
then separates into tributaries of fringe.

She seems unaware of that darkness
focused as she is on her craft
but near the middle finger, right hand
a touch of red, as if her very blood
has seeped beyond the protective thimble
and flows into the fabric of her art.

THE SECRET GARDEN
Illustrations by Tasha Tudor

Sorrow fills her, the way
moss fills the cracks of a long-forgotten
path. She pulls back the shelter
of ivy, the clutch of deep-rooted
grief, kneels in a secluded garden,
fingers stained with rust of loss.
The green there, cosseted in a bulb's
womb, makes its way to light, blossoms
in a barren space.

We are saved by many things:
a convent of silence, the grit
of experience, how a flute's
silver note penetrates the secret,
and a crow can bear our blackness.

ART NOUVEAU

Dragonfly
Wood Block Print
Francy Blumhagen

Night, and the dragonfly
in the block print near the bed
flies into dreamy abstraction
its webbed wings mysterious
blue-black iridescence,
like a veil of moonlight
wafting through darkness.

Stitched into European folktales
as the devil's darning needle
troll's spindle
adder's servant;
a shadowy, flashing stylet
despised and feared.

It alights on a temple bell
in a Kobe garden,
the wings, like mantilla lace,
brush the bright face
of a sunflower in Oaxaca.
Here a mark of renewal,
courage and strength,
this double-barred cross
rests with wings open.

What is it we expect
of our vulnerability?

A DEPARTURE ON NIGHTHAWKS

Oil on canvas, 1942
Edward Hopper 1882 - 1967
The Institute of Art, Chicago

When sleep does not come easy
and silence is a ballroom of ideas,
wild notions dancing round and round,
the decent cavorting with the *whys*
and *what ifs*, these crude dancers,
oblivious to the rhythms of life
and the music that keeps us dancing,
these step-on-toes partners that keep whirling,
imposers of bone crunching pain.

And at the center of it all
the dark night gathers silvered
confetti, reflections spinning
from this multifaceted ball
this earth, revealing
dappled images of other dancers,
almost touching, turning
in paired steps with our own,
nighthawks, separate, alone.

A GRAY DAY

Oil on Canvas, 1910 - 1911
Richard Emil Miller 1875 - 1943
National Academy of Design, NY

The woman could not be more beautiful;
upswept hair, flushed cheeks, delicate fingers
poised above tea cup, long, white dress
and periwinkle shawl; a candle burning blue.

She sits in a sheltered garden
near a table covered with sprigged cloth,
jug of milk and flowers
on a hand painted tray.

Her feet rest on a footstool
and beyond her a quiet pool;
all composed comfort.
Even the branch that extends

to the center of the scene belongs.
Apples dangle like polished jewels,
the largest one before the woman's eyes.
She looks down, perhaps unaware,

perhaps unwilling to see
how the branch, timelessly
suspended, casts
endless shades of gray.

THE ROOM OF FLOWERS

Oil on Canvas, 1894
Childe Hassam, 1859 - 1935
Private Collection

He paints Celia Thaxter's gardens again
and again, the delirious poppies, a field of red
flows to the shore of Appledore Island,
meets blue waters and white sails
like a bold American flag.

And now this jumbled room.
Constellations of flowers placed
among stacks of books; wanton
clutches of lilies, larkspur,
coreopsis, roses, for-get-me-nots.

Art covers the walls, ordered disorder,
as if the world turns in on itself here
where the coterie gather; Emerson,
Hawthorne, Longfellow…

Beyond books and golden lilies,
the woman in ruffled pink dress
reclines on the sofa reading
like a delicate peony discovered
in the garden.

Soon friends will gather
her flowers,
heap them around her coffin.

GARDEN SCENE

Abstract watercolor on paper, 2007
John Ringen, 1928 -
Private Collection

You can almost hear chords
of color descend into the garden,
from the thrum of hummingbird wings.

Delphinium's saturated blue beam,
Cerinthe oozing violet blood,
monarda's inferno.

The bird dips and lifts
above purple flames
of penstemon and salvia.

You don't need to see it to know
crickets fiddle an old-world tune
against the tremolo of bees.

Rest, you want only to feel
the curious beat and rhythm
of growth.

Trust me,
a watering can waits
beside the garden chair.

HILL ROAD
Watercolor on Paper, 2008
Glen Oberg, 1930 -
Poet's Collection

He thinks he's seen some visible trace of some absent thing.
Evanescence, from Different Hours by Stephen Dunn

On the wall above my desk
the painting; an historic
farmhouse, out buildings,
fields in light and shadow,
birds like quarter notes
along the telephone line;
a soft palette, purples,
greens, yellows and blues.

At first barely noticed,
a bit of it; fiery,
absolute red.
There a burning bush,
geraniums at the bottom
of porch steps and clustered
in a window box;
tail lights of an old truck.
Further out, near the tree line,
red that does not claim itself

yet it's there, sure of its need
to be, like a flash of anger
that excites the eye;
a visible trace
of some absent thing.

FARMER'S MARKET
Opaque Watercolor on paperboard, 1941
Mark Tobey, 1890 - 1976
Seattle Art Museum, Seattle Washington

If you could sign your name to moonlight
that is the thing, his dream-light of attainment,
how it swept over the bawdy house at First and Pike,
glared into the eyes of those who favored stacking

cars on that corner where the farmers gathered.
The light struck the metal table as he drank his morning
an irascible face nearly as angular as his painting,
the troikas of farmer, patron, market; artist, viewer, art.

He shouldered in to save the market, more interesting
than Paris stalls, the markets of London, Mexico, and China,
he said, and he wove his spectacular triangular web,
the people clustered in three-angled form, pyramids of style,

watercolor as if dipped from stippled Elliott Bay, ebbed
to harvest grown from the loam of Rainier Valley
and the bottomlands, swelled back to the city's belly
satisfying its hunger, his fertile vision.

A SUNDAY ON LA GRANDE JATTE

Oil on canvas, 1884 - 86
George Seurat 1859 - 91
The Art Institute, Chicago

Marbles cradled in the hand
scatter into a sheen of silence.
Only the spherical colors shout
as children play, the spangle
of their laughter swept
into quiet contemplation
by the tip of the brush.
Such silence.

Bugle notes
swallowed by a gentle sky
and the rustle of fashionable bustles
rounded in soundless elegance.
Small whirls of color create a universe
that tricks the eye, hoodwinks
even the monkey into harmonious
stillness.

INDIANS IN THE FOG

Charcoal on Paper, 1965
Brian Edstrom, 1961 -
Private Collection

Two smiling Indians paddle a canoe.
Nearby a gator swims in stylized waves,

returns a friendly grin. A quick sweep of the artist's hand
across charcoaled paper has caused a sudden shift

in weather. Only a duck flying through clouds
seems dissatisfied with its progress.

Four years old, he's on to new adventures.
Swift pencil strokes explore jungles,

scale graphite mountains where volleys
of mountain men wield black powder rifles,

enter the caves of whimsical dragons
that curl around uncertain treasure.

Now come the Noggas. Bald, baggy creatures
who sit atop telephone poles, need a shave, smoke cigars.

Soon he will sketch his vision, miscalculate,
begin again, draw his own conclusions;

Noggas, like hovering angels, perch on his bedposts.

HOW MANY SUNS

Monet's Garden at Vetheuil
Oil on canvas, 1880
Claude Monet, 1840 - 1926
National Gallery of Art, Washington D.C.

A small child, I glimpsed an instant
of infinity, followed the thought
along, speeding past stars and galaxies
until I feared I would travel forever,
disappear.

Now this young boy frocked in blue,
corn silk hair, child of sky and garden
stands on a shadowed path surrounded
by sunflowers, seed orbs like planets,
sprouting golden flames.

Does he ask the artist-father where the path
leads, what is beyond what's seen,
what makes the sky so irresistibly blue
you want to wing into its nothingness
sure you will find an answer?

The young know about questions,
how to fly beyond boundaries,
how beauty rises from the earth,
makes light into a whisper
of blue shadows.

ACKNOWLEDGMENTS

Grateful acknowledgment is made to the editors of the following journals where these poems first appeared.

American Gothic, First Place and Benefactors Award, Whidbey Island Writer's Conference, 2006; first appeared on Whidbey Island Writer's Association web site, 2006; Soundings Review, premiere edition, 2008

Private Man, Borderlands: Texas Poetry Review, 2009

The Gleaners, Floating Bridge Review, 2010

Green Apple on Black Plate, Hackney National Literary Award, third place, 2007; Washington Poet's Association literary journal, Cascade, premiere edition, 2007; Birmingham Arts Journal, 2008

Edward Hopper's Women, Connecticut River Review, 2011

Special thanks to Lorraine Healy and my poet friends for insightful critique and rich conversations.

.

Bio:

Lois Parker Edstrom is a freelance writer whose poetry has appeared in the *Birmingham Arts Journal, Borderlands: Texas Poetry Review, Floating Bridge Review, Clackamas Review,* and *Connecticut River Review,* among others. She has received two Hackney National Literary Awards, an Artist's International Award, and the Benefactor's Award from the Whidbey Island Writer's Conference. Her poetry has been adapted to dance and performed by the Bellingham Repertory Dance Company. She is the author of a previous chapbook, *What Brings Us to Water* which received the Poetica Publishing Company Chapbook Award, 2010. She lives on an island off the coast of Washington.

www.ingramcontent.com/pod-product-compliance
Ingram Content Group UK Ltd.
Pitfield, Milton Keynes, MK11 3LW, UK
UKHW041901190726
13854UKWH00003B/1022

9 781105 524233